ISBN: 9798883969019
Imprint: Independently published

Cover design by: Art Painter
Library of Congress Control Number: 2018675309
Printed in the United States of America

"In the symphony of ones and zeros, where the digital dance meets the human heartbeat, we navigate the melody of innovation, weaving stories that resonate through the binary tapestry of our interconnected world. In the embrace of technology, let curiosity be our compass, resilience our rhythm, and Digital Mastery the harmonious refrain guiding us through the ever-evolving composition of our digital odyssey."

CHIMEZIE IGWE

CONTENTS

Concert

PREFACE

Embarking on a Digital Odyssey

Welcome, dear reader, to a voyage through the realms of Digital Mastery. In an era where every click echoes with potential, where algorithms dance and ideas spark in the luminous glow of screens, this exploration beckons you to join a journey of discovery, innovation, and the artful mastery of technology in our lives.

As we set sail through these digital waters, the purpose is not just to navigate the waves of innovation but to uncover the stories that shape the digital landscape. In this preface, let us embark on a brief introduction to the heart of our odyssey, embracing the spirit of curiosity and the anticipation of what lies beyond the horizon of each page.

Setting the Course: The Digital Landscape Unveiled

The preface opens with a glimpse into the vast and ever-evolving digital landscape. In a tone that marries technology with familiarity, we'll lay the groundwork for an expedition into the intricacies of Digital Mastery. Engaging narratives will serve as a compass, guiding readers through the various facets of technology's impact on our lives, from personal moments to global shifts.

Navigating the Narrative: Stories that Illuminate

This section introduces the guiding principle of storytelling woven throughout the exploration. Stories become our guides, illuminating the complex intersections of technology and humanity. In a friendly tone, we'll explore how narratives create bridges between the digital and the personal, allowing readers to connect with the experiences, challenges, and triumphs of individuals and organizations navigating the digital realm.

The Spirit of Digital Mastery: A Harmonious Blend

Here, we delve into the essence of Digital Mastery—a harmonious blend of technology and human-centric values. In a tech and friendly tone, we'll explore the overarching theme that runs through the narrative, celebrating the ways in which individuals and entities not only adapt to technology but also shape it to align with human needs, ethics, and aspirations.

A Call to the Reader: Joining the Odyssey

The preface concludes with a call to the reader—an invitation to join this digital odyssey with open minds and curious hearts. In a friendly exploration, we'll convey the excitement of venturing into uncharted territories, where each turn of the page holds the promise of a new insight, a fresh perspective, or a captivating story. Engaging narratives will echo the sentiment that, in this exploration, the reader becomes an active participant in the ongoing narrative of Digital Mastery.

As we turn the digital page to commence this odyssey, let the preface serve as a compass, aligning our intentions and setting the course for a journey that illuminates the intricate dance between humanity and technology. May this exploration inspire, inform, and spark a curiosity that resonates long after the digital echoes fade. Welcome aboard, fellow traveler, to the captivating realms of

Digital Mastery.

CHAPTER 1
The Digital Dawn: Embracing Tech's Friendly Face

In the tapestry of our daily lives, technology weaves a vibrant thread, shaping the way we connect, work, and thrive. As we embark on this journey into the realm of Digital Mastery, let's step into the digital dawn together, where the language of technology speaks not in complexities, but in the friendly tones of innovation.

UNLOCKING THE DIGITAL LANGUAGE

Imagine standing at the threshold of a new era where technology isn't a distant entity but a companion, eager to simplify our lives. In this chapter, we'll unravel the digital language, breaking down jargon into digestible bits. From megabytes to algorithms, let's explore these digital building blocks, demystifying the language that powers our interconnected world.

THE TECH EVOLUTION THROUGH NARRATIVES

Every piece of technology has a story to tell—a narrative of evolution, adaptation, and transformative impact. From the humble beginnings of the first personal computer to the seamless integration of artificial intelligence into our daily routines, we'll journey through these narratives. It's not just about gadgets and codes; it's about the tales of innovation that have shaped the friendly face of tech we see today.

INSIGHTS FROM THE PIONEERS

Alongside engaging narratives, let's draw insights from the pioneers who paved the way for the digital landscape we navigate. We'll delve into the stories of visionaries who dared to dream beyond the confines of convention. What inspired them? What hurdles did they overcome? By peering into the past, we glean valuable insights that illuminate the path forward.

FROM ONES AND ZEROS TO HUMAN REALITIES

As we unravel the digital tapestry, it's crucial to remember that behind every line of code and every byte of data, there's a human touch. Let's explore how technology, often portrayed as a faceless entity, is, in fact, a reflection of human ingenuity and aspirations. We'll examine the ways in which tech mirrors our desires for connection, efficiency, and progress.

THE RISE OF USER-FRIENDLY TECH

Gone are the days of intimidating interfaces and complex commands. In the friendly face of tech, user experience takes center stage. We'll delve into the evolution of user-friendly technology, exploring how designs have shifted from being user-tolerant to user-centric. From intuitive apps to voice-activated assistants, we'll witness the revolution of tech that speaks our language.

DIGITAL EMPOWERMENT

Beyond the glossy screens and sleek devices, technology holds the power to empower. In this chapter, we'll uncover how digital tools have become instruments of empowerment, leveling the playing field for individuals and businesses alike. From online learning platforms to small businesses thriving in the digital marketplace, we'll witness the democratization of opportunities.

THE HUMAN SIDE OF DATA

In the digital landscape, data often takes center stage, but let's not forget the human side of this equation. We'll explore how data, when harnessed responsibly, can enhance our lives. From personalized recommendations to healthcare innovations, we'll discover how data becomes a force for good when guided by ethical considerations.

THE TECH-FRIENDLY FUTURE

As we wrap up this chapter, let's cast our gaze into the horizon of possibilities. What does the future hold in this tech-friendly world? We'll explore emerging technologies, from augmented reality to the Internet of Things, that promise to further integrate technology into the fabric of our lives. It's not just about the future of tech; it's about the future we shape with technology by our side.

In the friendly embrace of technology, this chapter invites you to become fluent in the language of the digital dawn. From insights drawn from the pioneers to the human stories behind the code, let's embark on this journey with curiosity and open hearts. The digital age isn't a destination; it's a continuous exploration, and together, we'll navigate the friendly face of technology that shapes our world.

CHAPTER 2
The Foundations of Digital Mastery

In the symphony of business and technology, Chapter 2 invites you to embark on a journey through the foundational keystones that lay the groundwork for Digital Mastery. It's not just about understanding the intricate language of technology; it's about dancing with the dynamic rhythm of digital transformation. So, tighten your virtual laces and let's traverse the digital landscape together.

DECIPHERING THE DIGITAL ALPHABET

Imagine the digital realm as a vast alphabet, where each letter represents a key technological concept. From APIs to UX/UI, our journey begins by decoding this digital alphabet. In a tech and friendly tone, we'll explore the language of technology, demystifying acronyms, and unraveling the code that shapes the digital experience. Consider this your tech dictionary, where the language of the digital domain becomes accessible to all.

NAVIGATING THE DIGITAL TRANSFORMATION ODYSSEY

As we step into the vibrant narratives of companies navigating the digital transformation odyssey, envision the digital landscape not as uncharted territory but as a canvas of endless possibilities. Engaging narratives will guide us through the metamorphosis of businesses—how they embraced change, adapted to challenges, and emerged resilient in the face of digital disruption. These stories are not just tales; they are blueprints for businesses aspiring to chart their course in the digital age.

INSIGHTS FROM DIGITAL PIONEERS

In the friendly hum of innovation, digital pioneers share insights that serve as lanterns in the dark, illuminating the path forward. Let's hear from those who have not only embraced digital transformation but have sculpted it into a catalyst for success. Valuable insights will be drawn from their experiences—lessons etched in the digital chronicles that businesses can leverage in their quest for mastery.

THE HUMAN TOUCH IN TECHNOLOGY

Beyond the lines of code and the circuits of hardware, let's acknowledge the human touch in technology. In a tech-friendly tone, we'll explore how technology isn't just a tool; it's an extension of our human capabilities. Dive into narratives where technology augments human potential, creating a synergy that goes beyond mere functionality. Here, technology becomes a friendly companion in the human journey.

USER EXPERIENCE: MORE THAN A BUZZWORD

In the digital world, user experience isn't a mere buzzword; it's the heartbeat of technology. With engaging narratives, we'll witness how businesses, in a tech and friendly tone, prioritize user-centric design. From intuitive interfaces to delightful experiences, technology evolves into a friendly companion that understands and responds to human needs. The narrative here is not just about functionality; it's about crafting digital experiences that resonate with users on a personal level.

DATA: THE DIGITAL GOLDMINE

Enter the digital goldmine—data. In a tech and friendly exploration, we'll uncover the richness of data-driven decision-making. It's not about drowning in data lakes; it's about extracting valuable insights that fuel informed choices. Engaging narratives will showcase how businesses, in their quest for Digital Mastery, harness the power of data analytics, machine learning, and AI to navigate the complexities of the digital landscape.

STRATEGIES FOR TECH HARMONY

Digital Mastery isn't a solo act; it's an orchestra of seamless integration. With rich content, we'll explore strategies that go beyond adopting the latest tech trends. From supply chain digitization to cultural shifts within organizations, envision businesses harmonizing technology into every facet of their operations. The narrative here is not just about tech adoption; it's about cultivating a tech-friendly mindset that permeates the organizational culture.

EVOLUTION OF CYBERSECURITY: FROM LOCKS TO ALGORITHMS

In a world where every bit is precious, cybersecurity becomes the digital guardian. Engaging narratives will unfold the evolution of cybersecurity strategies—from traditional locks to sophisticated algorithms. The narrative here is not about the fear of cyber threats; it's about the proactive measures businesses take to safeguard their digital assets. In tech and friendly exploration, envision cybersecurity not as a barrier but as an enabler of digital resilience.

CHAMPIONING DIGITAL LITERACY AND SKILLS

In a tech-savvy era, empowerment comes through digital literacy and skills development. Engaging narratives will spotlight initiatives that bridge the digital divide. From educational programs to upskilling endeavors, businesses become architects of a future where digital literacy is universal. The narrative here is not about technological elitism; it's about democratizing access to digital knowledge and skills.

CONCLUSION: SETTING SAIL INTO THE DIGITAL HORIZON

As we conclude this chapter, envision yourself equipped with the foundational knowledge essential for Digital Mastery. It's not just about understanding the digital alphabet; it's about composing a symphony where technology and business dance in harmony. The journey ahead promises a digital horizon filled with opportunities, challenges, and the friendly hum of innovation. As businesses set sail into the digital realm, armed with tech-friendly insights, the chapters ahead will further illuminate the path toward a future where technology is not just a tool but a trusted ally in the pursuit of mastery.

CHAPTER 3
Innovations Shaping the Future

As we navigate the terrain of Digital Mastery, Chapter 3 invites you into the vibrant world of innovations that shape the future. In a tech and friendly tone, this chapter delves into the transformative technologies propelling us toward a horizon where possibilities are as boundless as our imagination.

ARTIFICIAL INTELLIGENCE AND MACHINE LEARNING

Imagine a future where machines not only perform tasks but also learn and adapt. In a tech-friendly exploration, we'll unravel the tapestry of Artificial Intelligence (AI) and Machine Learning (ML). Engaging narratives will showcase how businesses harness the power of algorithms to analyze data, make predictions, and continuously improve. The narrative here is not about machines replacing humans but about a collaboration where human intelligence guides the evolution of artificial counterparts.

INTERNET OF THINGS (IOT) REVOLUTION

Step into a realm where everyday objects are interconnected, communicating seamlessly to enhance our lives. In a friendly exploration of the Internet of Things (IoT), envision a world where devices, from smart homes to industrial machinery, collaborate to create efficiencies. Engaging narratives will illuminate the transformative impact of IoT in diverse sectors, showcasing not just the technological prowess but the real-world benefits experienced by individuals and businesses.

BLOCKCHAIN TECHNOLOGY: BEYOND CRYPTOCURRENCIES

In a tech and friendly tone, let's demystify Blockchain, a technology extending beyond cryptocurrencies. Engaging narratives will unravel the potential of decentralized ledgers in ensuring transparency, security, and trust in various industries. Beyond the financial realm, envision Blockchain as a tool for enhancing supply chain transparency, streamlining healthcare data, and revolutionizing the way we authenticate information.

QUANTUM COMPUTING: A GLIMPSE INTO THE FUTURE

Prepare to be transported into the future with Quantum Computing. In a tech-friendly exploration, we'll delve into the principles of quantum mechanics that promise to revolutionize computation. Engaging narratives will unfold the potential applications of quantum computing, from solving complex problems in seconds to transforming industries like finance, healthcare, and logistics. The narrative here is not just about computational power but about the profound impact on problem-solving in the digital age.

AUGMENTED REALITY (AR) AND VIRTUAL REALITY (VR)

Step into the immersive worlds of Augmented Reality (AR) and Virtual Reality (VR), where digital and physical realities converge. In a friendly exploration, envision applications that go beyond gaming—AR aiding in navigation, VR transforming training simulations, and both redefining the way we experience entertainment. Engaging narratives will showcase how these technologies are not just changing how we see the world but also how we interact with it.

BIOTECHNOLOGY AND GENETIC ENGINEERING

In a tech and friendly tone, let's journey into the realm of Biotechnology and Genetic Engineering. Engaging narratives will unveil the innovations that redefine healthcare, agriculture, and environmental sustainability. From CRISPR technology editing genes to synthetic biology creating bio-inspired solutions, envision a future where our understanding of life sciences reshapes the very fabric of our existence.

ROBOTICS: AUTOMATING THE FUTURE

Picture a world where robots are not just mechanical entities but collaborative companions. In a tech-friendly exploration, we'll uncover the evolution of robotics, from assembly lines to collaborative robots (cobots). Engaging narratives will showcase how robotics is enhancing efficiency, productivity, and safety across industries. The narrative here is not about robots replacing human jobs but about a partnership that amplifies human capabilities.

DRONES: NAVIGATING THE SKIES OF INNOVATION

In a friendly exploration of the skies, envision drones as versatile tools transforming industries. Engaging narratives will showcase how drones go beyond recreational use, aiding in agriculture, disaster response, and even last-mile delivery. The narrative here is not just about aerial gadgets but about the practical applications that make them indispensable in various fields.

3D PRINTING: CRAFTING THE FUTURE LAYER BY LAYER

In a tech and friendly tone, let's explore the realm of 3D Printing. Engaging narratives will unveil the transformative power of layer-by-layer construction, from manufacturing prototypes to creating personalized medical implants. The narrative here is not just about printing objects but about a technology that democratizes manufacturing, fostering innovation in unforeseen ways.

RENEWABLE ENERGY INNOVATIONS

As we shift gears to a sustainable future, renewable energy innovations take center stage. In a tech-friendly exploration, envision a world powered by solar, wind, and other sustainable sources. Engaging narratives will unfold the advancements in energy storage, grid management, and the integration of renewables into our daily lives. The narrative here is not just about green energy but about a paradigm shift toward a sustainable and tech-driven energy future.

CONCLUSION: A TAPESTRY OF TECHNOLOGICAL EVOLUTION

As we conclude this chapter, envision a tapestry woven with the threads of technological evolution. It's not just a glimpse into the future; it's an invitation to be part of the innovations shaping our world. In a tech and friendly tone, the journey ahead promises a landscape where these technologies don't just exist in isolation but converge to create a future that is both extraordinary and accessible. As we continue our exploration of Digital Mastery, each innovation becomes a brushstroke, contributing to the masterpiece of a tech-friendly future where technology enhances the human experience.

CHAPTER 4
Nurturing Digital Competence in a Tech-Friendly World

Welcome to the heart of Digital Mastery, where Chapter 4 delves into the vital realm of Digital Literacy and Skills Development. In a tech and friendly tone, this chapter unfolds as a guide to navigating the landscapes of knowledge in the digital age. Join us on a journey that not only explores the importance of digital literacy but also delves into the strategies for skills development, fostering a community of tech-savvy individuals ready to thrive in the digital era.

THE ESSENCE OF DIGITAL LITERACY

Imagine digital literacy not as a skill set confined to the tech-savvy but as a universal language spoken by all. In a tech-friendly exploration, we'll unravel the essence of digital literacy, showcasing its importance in the interconnected world we inhabit. Engaging narratives will illustrate how digital literacy is not just about knowing how to use devices but understanding the broader implications of technology in our personal and professional lives.

FROM NOVICE TO NAVIGATOR: A PERSONAL DIGITAL JOURNEY

Embark on a personal digital journey—a narrative that resonates with individuals at various stages of their digital literacy. In a friendly tone, we'll explore stories of novices transforming into digital navigators. Whether it's learning to use social media, mastering online tools, or understanding the basics of coding, these personal narratives will inspire readers to embrace their own digital evolution.

DIGITAL INCLUSION: BRIDGING THE DIVIDE

In a world where technology is ubiquitous, digital inclusion becomes a social imperative. Engaging narratives will highlight initiatives that bridge the digital divide, ensuring that access to technology and digital literacy is not a privilege but a right. The narrative here is not just about providing devices and internet access; it's about fostering an inclusive environment where everyone has the opportunity to participate in the digital revolution.

STRATEGIES FOR ENHANCING DIGITAL LITERACY

Transitioning into strategies for enhancing digital literacy, this section explores actionable insights for individuals and communities. In a tech and friendly exploration, envision a roadmap that includes user-friendly tutorials, interactive learning platforms, and community-driven initiatives. Engaging narratives will showcase how communities, schools, and organizations are taking proactive steps to empower individuals with the skills needed to navigate the digital landscape confidently.

THE ROLE OF SCHOOLS IN FOSTERING DIGITAL LITERACY

Schools play a pivotal role in shaping the digital acumen of future generations. In a friendly exploration, we'll delve into narratives of innovative educational approaches that integrate digital literacy into the curriculum. Engaging stories will highlight how educators leverage technology to create dynamic learning experiences, preparing students not just for exams but for the demands of a tech-driven future.

UPSKILLING AND RESKILLING FOR THE DIGITAL WORKFORCE

The digital era demands a workforce equipped with ever-evolving skills. In a tech-friendly exploration, we'll unravel narratives of professionals who embraced upskilling and reskilling to stay relevant in their careers. From online courses to immersive boot camps, these stories illustrate the transformative power of continuous learning in the face of technological advancements.

DIGITAL LITERACY FOR OLDER GENERATIONS: A GENTLE TRANSITION

In a friendly tone, let's explore the narratives of older generations navigating the digital landscape. Engaging stories will highlight the importance of providing tailored support and creating spaces where seniors can comfortably enhance their digital literacy. The narrative here is not about imposing technology but about facilitating a gentle transition, ensuring that everyone, regardless of age, can harness the benefits of the digital age.

EMPOWERING ENTREPRENEURS WITH DIGITAL SKILLS

Entrepreneurship in the digital age requires a unique set of skills. In a tech-friendly exploration, envision narratives of entrepreneurs who embraced digital literacy to drive their ventures forward. Engaging stories will showcase how small businesses and startups leverage digital tools for marketing, e-commerce, and data analytics, illustrating the transformative impact of digital skills on business success.

THE INTERSECTION OF CREATIVITY AND DIGITAL LITERACY

In the creative realm, digital literacy becomes a canvas for innovation. In a friendly exploration, we'll unravel the narratives of artists, writers, and creators who seamlessly integrate digital tools into their craft. Engaging stories will showcase how creativity flourishes in the digital age, transcending traditional boundaries and opening new avenues for expression.

DIGITAL LITERACY FOR SOCIAL IMPACT

Digital literacy isn't just a personal skill; it's a catalyst for social impact. In a tech and friendly exploration, we'll delve into narratives of individuals and organizations leveraging digital literacy for community development, advocacy, and social change. Engaging stories will illustrate how the ripple effect of digital literacy extends beyond individuals, creating positive transformations on a broader scale.

CONCLUSION: A COMMUNITY OF DIGITAL NAVIGATORS

As we conclude this chapter, envision a community of digital navigators—individuals who not only possess digital literacy but actively contribute to the collective growth in a tech-friendly world. The journey into Digital Mastery extends beyond mastering tools; it's about fostering a mindset of continuous learning, adaptability, and inclusivity. With rich content and engaging narratives, this chapter serves as a guide, inspiring readers to embark on their unique digital journeys, equipped with the skills and literacy needed to thrive in the dynamic landscape of the digital era.

CHAPTER 6
Symphony of Success - The Intersection of Business and Technology

In the dynamic tapestry of Digital Mastery, Chapter 6 unravels the intricate dance between business and technology—a symphony of success where innovation, strategy, and human-centric approaches harmonize to propel organizations into the future. This chapter adopts a tech and friendly tone, weaving engaging narratives, valuable insights, and rich content to illuminate the interconnected world of business and technology. Join us on a journey where the boundaries blur and the fusion of these realms creates a melody of progress.

THE EVOLUTIONARY OVERTURE: BUSINESS AND TECHNOLOGY IN CONCERT

Envision the opening notes of our symphony—an exploration into the evolutionary overture of business and technology.

The intricate dance between business and technology has shaped the digital landscape, creating a harmonious symphony of progress. In this chapter, we delve into the evolutionary overture, exploring the intertwined history of these two realms. In a tech and friendly tone, let's journey through the milestones that have defined the collaboration between business and technology, setting the stage for the symphony of success.

INCEPTION: FROM MAINFRAMES TO MICROCHIPS

Our narrative begins with the inception of technology in business, from the era of mainframes to the advent of microchips. Engaging stories will unfold how businesses embraced emerging technologies, transforming operations and opening new frontiers. The friendly exploration will highlight the pioneers who saw the potential of technology not just as a tool but as a catalyst for growth.

STRATEGIC CRESCENDO: THE RISE OF DIGITAL TRANSFORMATION

As we move through the symphony, a strategic crescendo emerges—the rise of digital transformation. In a tech-friendly exploration, we'll unravel narratives of businesses adopting digital strategies that transcend traditional boundaries. Engaging stories will showcase how organizations, driven by a vision of the future, leverage technology to enhance customer experiences, streamline operations, and stay ahead in an ever-evolving market.

INNOVATIVE COUNTERPOINT: DISRUPTION AND ADAPTATION

The symphony takes an unexpected turn with the innovative counterpoint of disruption and adaptation. In a friendly tone, we'll explore stories of businesses facing technological disruptions, from the dot-com boom to the mobile revolution. Engaging narratives will illustrate how successful organizations not only weathered these storms but also adapted, emerging stronger and more resilient.

COLLABORATIVE CRESCENDO: THE ECOSYSTEM OF PARTNERSHIPS

In the tech and friendly landscape, collaborative crescendos echo through the narrative—the ecosystem of partnerships. Engaging stories will showcase how businesses, big and small, form symbiotic relationships with technology providers, startups, and other organizations. The narrative here is not just about transactions but about collaborative ventures that propel innovation and mutual growth.

HUMAN-CENTRIC MELODY: USER EXPERIENCE AND EMPATHY

Amidst the technological intricacies, a human-centric melody emerges—the importance of user experience and empathy in the symphony. In a friendly exploration, we'll unravel narratives that emphasize how successful businesses prioritize the user journey. Engaging stories will showcase how a deep understanding of human needs and emotions drives the design and implementation of technology, fostering a connection that goes beyond functionality.

AGILE RHYTHMS: NAVIGATING CHANGE WITH FLEXIBILITY

The symphony encounters agile rhythms—a reflection of businesses navigating change with flexibility. In a tech and friendly tone, we'll explore stories of organizations that embrace agility as a core principle. Engaging narratives will highlight how the ability to pivot, innovate, and adapt to changing landscapes becomes a competitive advantage in the dynamic interplay between business and technology.

DATA HARMONIES: LEVERAGING INSIGHTS FOR STRATEGIC DECISIONS

As we progress through the symphony, data harmonies resonate—a celebration of businesses leveraging insights for strategic decisions. In a friendly exploration, we'll unravel narratives of organizations harnessing the power of data analytics, artificial intelligence, and machine learning. Engaging stories will showcase how data becomes not just a resource but a guiding force in shaping business strategies.

ETHICAL REFRAINS: THE HARMONY OF BUSINESS AND SOCIAL RESPONSIBILITY

In the tech and friendly landscape, ethical refrains echo through the narrative—the harmony of business and social responsibility. Engaging stories will showcase businesses that intertwine success with a commitment to social and environmental causes. The narrative here is not just about profit margins but about organizations recognizing their role in creating a positive impact on society.

STRIKING A BALANCE: THE CONDUCTOR'S DILEMMA

The symphony reaches its zenith, posing the conductor's dilemma—striking a balance between innovation and responsibility. In a friendly exploration, we'll unravel narratives that showcase how successful organizations find the delicate equilibrium between pushing technological boundaries and ensuring ethical business practices. Engaging stories will highlight the leaders who navigate this complex terrain, fostering a culture where innovation and responsibility coexist.

COLLATERAL CADENCE: LESSONS LEARNED AND FUTURE HARMONIES

As the symphony nears its conclusion, a collateral cadence emerges—lessons learned and future harmonies. Engaging narratives will reflect on the journey so far, extracting valuable insights from the intersection of business and technology. The friendly exploration will invite readers to envision the future harmonies—innovations, collaborations, and human-centric approaches that will shape the next movements in the symphony of success.

CONCLUSION: APPLAUSE AND ANTICIPATION FOR THE ENCORE

As we conclude this chapter, imagine the applause echoing through the auditorium of business and technology. In a tech and friendly tone, the journey into the intersection of these realms serves as both a celebration of achievements and a prelude to the encore. With rich content and engaging narratives, this chapter invites readers to anticipate the evolving symphony, where the collaboration between business and technology continues to create melodies of progress, innovation, and human-centric success.

CHAPTER 7
Navigating the Moral Compass - Ethical Considerations in the Digital Era

In the vast expanse of Digital Mastery, Chapter 7 embarks on a reflective journey, illuminating the crucial intersection of ethics and technology. This chapter adopts a tech and friendly tone, weaving engaging narratives, valuable insights, and rich content to explore the ethical considerations that arise in the digital era. Join us as we navigate the moral compass, contemplating the responsibilities and challenges woven into the fabric of our interconnected world.

INTRODUCTION: THE ETHICAL LANDSCAPE OF THE DIGITAL ERA

Set against the backdrop of the ever-expanding digital landscape, the introduction to this chapter invites readers into the ethical considerations that permeate our daily interactions with technology. In a tech and friendly tone, we'll explore the profound impact of digital advancements on our ethical framework, laying the groundwork for the nuanced discussions that follow.

THE HUMAN-CENTRIC APPROACH: PUTTING PEOPLE FIRST

At the heart of ethical considerations lies a human-centric approach. In a friendly exploration, we'll unravel narratives that underscore the importance of prioritizing people over technological objectives. Engaging stories will highlight instances where businesses, innovators, and policymakers consciously put human welfare at the forefront, ensuring that technology serves as a tool for empowerment rather than exploitation.

DATA ETHICS: BALANCING INNOVATION AND PRIVACY

As we navigate the digital landscape, data ethics emerges as a critical focal point. In a tech and friendly tone, we'll delve into narratives that explore the delicate balance between innovation and privacy. Engaging stories will showcase instances where organizations implement responsible data practices, respecting user privacy while leveraging data for positive advancements. The narrative here is not just about compliance but about an ethical commitment to data stewardship.

ALGORITHMIC ACCOUNTABILITY: UNMASKING BIAS AND FAIRNESS

In the tech-friendly exploration of algorithms, we confront the challenge of ensuring accountability. Engaging narratives will unravel stories that shed light on the biases embedded in algorithms and the ethical imperative to address these issues. The chapter will delve into instances where organizations actively work towards algorithmic fairness, acknowledging the responsibility to create technology that reflects the diversity and inclusivity of society.

DIGITAL INCLUSION AND ACCESSIBILITY: BRIDGING ETHICAL GAPS

Ethical considerations extend to ensuring digital inclusion and accessibility for all. In a friendly exploration, we'll delve into narratives that showcase efforts to bridge the digital divide, making technology accessible to diverse populations. Engaging stories will highlight initiatives that prioritize inclusivity, recognizing that ethical technology is not just about functionality but about ensuring equal opportunities for participation.

THE SOCIAL IMPACT OF TECHNOLOGY: NURTURING POSITIVE CHANGE

The digital era brings forth an ethical responsibility to harness technology for positive social impact. In a tech and friendly tone, we'll explore narratives that illustrate how businesses and individuals contribute to societal well-being through technology. Engaging stories will showcase instances where technology becomes a catalyst for positive change, addressing social challenges and fostering community empowerment.

CYBERSECURITY ETHICS: SAFEGUARDING WITH INTEGRITY

Ethical considerations permeate the realm of cybersecurity. In a friendly exploration, we'll unravel narratives that delve into the ethical dimensions of safeguarding digital spaces. Engaging stories will highlight instances where ethical cybersecurity practices not only protect against threats but also prioritize integrity, transparency, and accountability in the face of evolving digital risks.

TECH FOR GOOD: FOSTERING ETHICAL INNOVATION

The narrative turns to the concept of "Tech for Good," exploring how innovation can be harnessed ethically for the betterment of humanity. In a tech and friendly tone, we'll delve into narratives that showcase the transformative power of technology when aligned with ethical principles. Engaging stories will highlight instances where startups, corporations, and individuals contribute to societal well-being through innovative, ethical solutions.

ETHICAL LEADERSHIP IN THE DIGITAL AGE: SETTING THE TONE

Leadership plays a pivotal role in shaping ethical considerations within the digital landscape. In a friendly exploration, we'll unravel narratives that spotlight ethical leadership—individuals who set the tone for organizations, foster cultures of integrity, and navigate the complexities of ethical decision-making in a rapidly evolving digital age. Engaging stories will showcase instances where leaders prioritize ethical values, creating environments where innovation and integrity coexist.

PUBLIC POLICY AND ETHICAL FRAMEWORKS: SHAPING A RESPONSIBLE FUTURE

The chapter explores the role of public policy in shaping ethical frameworks for the digital era. In a tech and friendly tone, we'll delve into narratives that illustrate how policymakers, regulatory bodies, and governments contribute to the establishment of ethical guidelines. Engaging stories will showcase instances where ethical considerations are embedded in policy decisions, ensuring that technology evolves within a responsible and accountable framework.

THE DARK SIDE: NAVIGATING ETHICAL PITFALLS

As we navigate the ethical landscape, we confront the dark side—the ethical pitfalls that can arise in the digital era. In a friendly exploration, we'll unravel narratives that shed light on instances where technology has been misused or ethical considerations overlooked. Engaging stories will highlight the lessons learned from these pitfalls, emphasizing the importance of continuous ethical scrutiny in the development and deployment of technology.

CONCLUSION: GUIDING PRINCIPLES FOR AN ETHICAL TOMORROW

The chapter concludes by distilling guiding principles for an ethical tomorrow in the digital era. In a tech and friendly tone, we'll reflect on the narratives and insights shared throughout the exploration of ethical considerations. Engaging stories will leave readers with a sense of responsibility, urging them to contribute to the ongoing dialogue on ethics in technology and ensuring that the digital era evolves within a framework of integrity, empathy, and ethical mindfulness.

CHAPTER 8
Beyond the Horizon - Future Trends and Emerging Technologies

In the expansive landscape of Digital Mastery, Chapter 8 embarks on a journey into the future, casting a visionary gaze upon the evolving trends and emerging technologies that will shape the digital era. This chapter adopts a tech and friendly tone, weaving engaging narratives, valuable insights, and rich content to explore the exciting possibilities and potential challenges that lie beyond the horizon. Join us as we navigate the frontiers of innovation, anticipating the next wave of transformation in the ever-evolving digital landscape.

INTRODUCTION: A GLIMPSE INTO TOMORROW'S DIGITAL LANDSCAPE

The introduction sets the stage for an exploration into the uncharted territories of future trends and emerging technologies. In a tech and friendly tone, we'll embark on a journey that transcends the present, providing readers with a glimpse into the transformative possibilities that await in tomorrow's digital landscape.

AI AND MACHINE LEARNING: THE SYMPHONY OF INTELLIGENT AUTOMATION

At the forefront of future trends, artificial intelligence (AI) and machine learning compose a symphony of intelligent automation. In a friendly exploration, we'll unravel narratives that showcase the evolution of AI and machine learning, exploring how these technologies become integral to decision-making, problem-solving, and innovative advancements. Engaging stories will highlight instances where businesses leverage AI to enhance efficiency, personalize experiences, and unlock new frontiers of creativity.

IMMERSIVE TECHNOLOGIES: A TAPESTRY OF VIRTUAL AND AUGMENTED REALITIES

The narrative unfolds into the realm of immersive technologies, weaving a tapestry of virtual and augmented realities. In a tech and friendly tone, we'll delve into narratives that illustrate the transformative impact of immersive experiences on various industries. Engaging stories will showcase instances where virtual and augmented realities redefine education, entertainment, healthcare, and more, creating immersive landscapes that blur the lines between the digital and physical worlds.

5G AND CONNECTIVITY: THE ACCELERATED PULSE OF THE DIGITAL NERVOUS SYSTEM

The digital landscape accelerates with the advent of 5G and enhanced connectivity, becoming the nervous system that propels innovation forward. In a friendly exploration, we'll unravel narratives that showcase how 5G revolutionizes communication, connectivity, and the Internet of Things (IoT). Engaging stories will highlight instances where businesses leverage ultra-fast connectivity to enable real-time experiences, from smart cities to autonomous vehicles, ushering in a new era of seamless interconnectivity.

BLOCKCHAIN AND DECENTRALIZED TECHNOLOGIES: THE UNSEEN ARCHITECT OF TRUST

The narrative extends to the unseen architect of trust—blockchain and decentralized technologies. In a tech and friendly tone, we'll delve into narratives that illustrate how blockchain transforms industries by enhancing security, transparency, and trust in digital transactions. Engaging stories will showcase instances where decentralized technologies disrupt traditional models, from finance to supply chain, unlocking new possibilities for efficiency and integrity.

BIOTECHNOLOGY AND HEALTH TECH: NURTURING A REVOLUTION IN HEALTHCARE

A revolutionary wave emerges in healthcare through biotechnology and health tech. In a friendly exploration, we'll unravel narratives that showcase the transformative impact of these technologies on diagnostics, treatment, and personalized medicine. Engaging stories will highlight instances where biotechnology and health tech contribute to breakthroughs in disease prevention, precision medicine, and the democratization of healthcare access.

SUSTAINABLE TECH: BALANCING INNOVATION WITH ENVIRONMENTAL STEWARDSHIP

As the digital landscape evolves, sustainability takes center stage. In a tech and friendly tone, we'll delve into narratives that showcase how sustainable technologies become integral to business practices and innovation. Engaging stories will highlight instances where businesses prioritize environmental stewardship, leveraging sustainable tech to reduce carbon footprints, promote circular economies, and contribute to an eco-friendlier future.

QUANTUM COMPUTING: UNLOCKING THE SECRETS OF UNPRECEDENTED PROCESSING POWER

The narrative ventures into the realm of quantum computing, unlocking the secrets of unprecedented processing power. In a friendly exploration, we'll unravel narratives that showcase the potential of quantum computing to solve complex problems and revolutionize industries. Engaging stories will highlight instances where businesses harness quantum capabilities to accelerate research, optimize supply chains, and usher in a new era of computational possibilities.

EDGE COMPUTING: THE DECENTRALIZED ORCHESTRA OF DATA PROCESSING

A decentralized orchestra of data processing emerges with the rise of edge computing. In a tech and friendly tone, we'll delve into narratives that showcase how edge computing transforms the way data is processed, analyzed, and utilized. Engaging stories will highlight instances where businesses leverage edge computing to achieve low-latency, real-time decision-making, and enhanced efficiency in diverse applications, from smart cities to industrial IoT.

HUMAN AUGMENTATION: BRIDGING THE DIVIDE BETWEEN MAN AND MACHINE

The narrative explores the frontiers of human augmentation, bridging the divide between man and machine. In a friendly exploration, we'll unravel narratives that showcase how technologies enhance human capabilities, from exoskeletons and brain-computer interfaces to wearable devices. Engaging stories will highlight instances where human augmentation contributes to improved healthcare, increased accessibility, and innovative solutions for individuals with diverse abilities.

CYBERSECURITY IN THE FUTURE: SAFEGUARDING THE EVOLVING DIGITAL LANDSCAPE

The chapter delves into the future of cybersecurity, safeguarding the evolving digital landscape. In a tech and friendly tone, we'll unravel narratives that showcase how cybersecurity adapts to the challenges posed by emerging technologies. Engaging stories will highlight instances where businesses and individuals implement proactive cybersecurity measures to protect against evolving threats, ensuring a secure digital future.

CONCLUSION: PIONEERING THE DIGITAL FRONTIER

As we conclude this chapter, envision pioneering the digital frontier—a landscape where future trends and emerging technologies converge to shape the next era of Digital Mastery. In a tech and friendly tone, the exploration serves as a call to action, inviting readers to anticipate, embrace, and contribute to the transformative possibilities that lie ahead. With rich content and engaging narratives, this chapter sets the stage for a future where innovation, ethical considerations, and human-centric values intertwine to propel the digital landscape into uncharted territories.

CHAPTER 9
Digital Alchemy - Case Studies in Digital Mastery

In the enchanting tapestry of Digital Mastery, Chapter 9 unfolds as a collection of captivating case studies, each a testament to the transformative power of technology and innovation. This chapter adopts a tech and friendly tone, weaving engaging narratives, valuable insights, and rich content to explore real-world examples of organizations and individuals who have mastered the digital realm. Join us on a journey through these digital alchemists' stories, where challenges are turned into opportunities, and innovation becomes the key to unlocking success.

INTRODUCTION: UNVEILING THE DIGITAL ALCHEMISTS

The introduction sets the stage for the exploration of digital alchemy, introducing readers to the concept of organizations and individuals as modern-day alchemists. In a tech and friendly tone, we'll embark on a journey through case studies that reveal the secrets behind the transformation of challenges into digital gold.

CASE STUDY 1: TRANSFORMATIVE INNOVATION IN E-COMMERCE

Our first case study immerses us in the world of transformative innovation within the realm of e-commerce. Engaging narratives will unfold the story of an e-commerce giant that navigated challenges, embraced technological advancements, and redefined the online shopping experience. The friendly exploration will highlight strategies, technological integrations, and customer-centric approaches that propelled the organization to digital success.

CASE STUDY 2: RESILIENCE AND ADAPTATION IN A GLOBAL CRISIS

In this case study, we delve into a narrative of resilience and adaptation during a global crisis. In a tech and friendly tone, we'll explore how a multinational corporation navigated unprecedented challenges, leveraging digital tools and strategies to adapt swiftly. Engaging stories will showcase the agility, innovative thinking, and strategic decision-making that enabled the organization to not only weather the storm but emerge stronger in the face of adversity.

CASE STUDY 3: THE DIGITAL TRANSFORMATION OF TRADITIONAL INDUSTRIES

The narrative extends to the digital transformation of traditional industries, uncovering how age-old practices evolve with technology. In a friendly exploration, we'll unravel the story of a heritage industry that embraced digital innovation to stay relevant in the modern era. Engaging stories will showcase the harmonious blend of tradition and technology, illustrating how embracing digital tools revitalized the industry and expanded its reach.

CASE STUDY 4: FOSTERING A CULTURE OF INNOVATION IN STARTUPS

Venturing into the dynamic landscape of startups, this case study explores the importance of fostering a culture of innovation. In a tech and friendly tone, we'll delve into the narratives of a startup ecosystem that thrives on creativity, adaptability, and technological ingenuity. Engaging stories will highlight how a culture of innovation becomes the driving force behind startups' success, shaping their trajectory in the competitive digital arena.

CASE STUDY 5: BUILDING DIGITAL COMMUNITIES AND FANDOMS

The narrative unfolds into the realm of building digital communities and fandoms, exploring how organizations cultivate passionate online communities around their brands. In a friendly exploration, we'll unravel stories of companies that mastered the art of community engagement, leveraging technology to create immersive, inclusive spaces for their audiences. Engaging narratives will showcase the impact of digital fandoms on brand loyalty, marketing strategies, and overall business success.

CASE STUDY 6: REVOLUTIONIZING EDUCATION THROUGH EDTECH

In this case study, we immerse ourselves in the realm of education technology (EdTech), exploring how digital tools revolutionize the way we learn. In a tech and friendly tone, we'll unravel narratives that showcase the transformative power of EdTech platforms, from personalized learning experiences to global connectivity in education. Engaging stories will illustrate how technology becomes a catalyst for positive change in the educational landscape.

CASE STUDY 7: REDEFINING HEALTHCARE DELIVERY THROUGH TELEMEDICINE

The narrative extends to the redefinition of healthcare delivery through telemedicine, exploring how digital solutions bridge gaps in access to medical services. In a friendly exploration, we'll delve into narratives that highlight the adoption of telemedicine platforms, their impact on patient care, and the evolution of healthcare delivery in the digital age. Engaging stories will showcase how technology becomes a lifeline, providing healthcare access where traditional methods fall short.

CASE STUDY 8: THE SOCIAL IMPACT OF DIGITAL PHILANTHROPY

In this case study, we explore the social impact of digital philanthropy, unveiling stories of organizations and individuals leveraging technology for charitable causes. In a tech and friendly tone, we'll unravel narratives that showcase how digital platforms amplify the reach and effectiveness of philanthropic initiatives. Engaging stories will highlight the intersection of technology and empathy, demonstrating how digital philanthropy becomes a force for positive change.

CONCLUSION: LESSONS FROM THE DIGITAL ALCHEMISTS

As we conclude this chapter, envision the collective wisdom gleaned from the digital alchemists—the organizations and individuals who have mastered the art of Digital Mastery. In a tech and friendly tone, the lessons learned from these case studies become guiding principles for readers, offering insights into the strategies, innovations, and human-centric approaches that lead to success in the digital realm. With rich content and engaging narratives, this chapter serves as a source of inspiration and practical wisdom, inviting readers to apply the lessons of the digital alchemists in their journeys of transformation and innovation.

CHAPTER 10
Guiding through the Storm - Navigating the Challenges of Rapid Technological Change

In the ever-accelerating voyage of Digital Mastery, Chapter 10 stands as a beacon, guiding readers through the tempest of challenges brought about by rapid technological change. This chapter adopts a tech and friendly tone, weaving engaging narratives, valuable insights, and rich content to explore the hurdles and strategies in navigating the stormy seas of innovation. Join us on a journey through the challenges, lessons, and triumphs that accompany the relentless pace of technological evolution.

INTRODUCTION: THE TURBULENT SEAS OF TECHNOLOGICAL EVOLUTION

The introduction invites readers to embark on a voyage through the turbulent seas of technological evolution. In a tech and friendly tone, we'll set the stage for exploring the challenges that arise when navigating the swiftly changing currents of innovation. Engaging narratives will paint a vivid picture of the stormy landscape that organizations and individuals must navigate in the pursuit of Digital Mastery.

CHALLENGE 1: THE NEED FOR CONTINUOUS LEARNING AND SKILL EVOLUTION

The first challenge delves into the necessity for continuous learning and skill evolution in the face of rapid technological change. In a friendly exploration, we'll unravel narratives that underscore the importance of adaptability, upskilling, and embracing a growth mindset. Engaging stories will highlight instances where individuals and organizations successfully navigate the challenge of staying abreast of evolving technologies and fostering a culture of lifelong learning.

CHALLENGE 2: BALANCING INNOVATION WITH CYBERSECURITY

The narrative extends to the delicate balance between innovation and cybersecurity. In a tech and friendly tone, we'll explore stories of organizations that grapple with the challenge of protecting digital assets while pushing the boundaries of innovation. Engaging narratives will showcase instances where businesses implement robust cybersecurity measures without stifling creativity, ensuring a secure and innovative digital landscape.

CHALLENGE 3: ADDRESSING ETHICAL DILEMMAS IN TECHNOLOGY

The exploration continues into the realm of ethical dilemmas in technology. In a friendly exploration, we'll unravel narratives that delve into the challenges organizations face when navigating the ethical dimensions of rapidly advancing technologies. Engaging stories will highlight instances where businesses confront ethical dilemmas head-on, adopting frameworks and practices that align innovation with responsible and ethical considerations.

CHALLENGE 4: OVERCOMING RESISTANCE TO CHANGE

The narrative unfolds into the challenge of overcoming resistance to change, a common hurdle in the path of technological evolution. In a tech and friendly tone, we'll explore stories that showcase strategies employed by organizations to foster a culture of openness, adaptability, and resilience. Engaging narratives will highlight instances where leaders successfully navigate resistance, turning it into a catalyst for positive transformation.

CHALLENGE 5: ENSURING DIGITAL INCLUSIVITY AND ACCESSIBILITY

In this challenge, we explore the imperative of ensuring digital inclusivity and accessibility. In a friendly exploration, we'll unravel narratives that shed light on the obstacles faced by organizations striving to make technology accessible to diverse populations. Engaging stories will highlight instances where businesses prioritize inclusivity, leveraging technology to bridge gaps and create digital experiences that cater to a wide range of users.

CHALLENGE 6: NAVIGATING THE REGULATORY LANDSCAPE

The narrative ventures into the challenge of navigating the regulatory landscape that governs rapidly evolving technologies. In a tech and friendly tone, we'll explore stories of organizations grappling with the complexities of compliance, legal frameworks, and regulatory changes. Engaging narratives will showcase instances where businesses successfully navigate regulatory challenges, aligning their strategies with legal requirements while fostering innovation.

CHALLENGE 7: MANAGING DATA OVERLOAD AND PRIVACY CONCERNS

The exploration continues into the challenge of managing data overload and addressing privacy concerns. In a friendly exploration, we'll unravel narratives that showcase the struggles organizations face in handling vast amounts of data while respecting user privacy. Engaging stories will highlight instances where businesses implement robust data management practices, ensuring responsible and transparent use of information in the digital landscape.

CHALLENGE 8: FOSTERING COLLABORATION IN A DIGITALLY CONNECTED WORLD

In this challenge, we delve into the importance of fostering collaboration in a digitally connected world. In a tech and friendly tone, we'll explore stories that illustrate the challenges organizations face in creating collaborative environments across digital platforms. Engaging narratives will highlight instances where businesses leverage technology to enhance teamwork, communication, and innovation in the era of remote work and global connectivity.

CONCLUSION: NAVIGATIONAL WISDOM IN THE DIGITAL STORM

As we conclude this chapter, envision the navigational wisdom gained in traversing the challenges of rapid technological change. In a tech and friendly tone, the lessons learned from these narratives become guiding principles for readers, offering insights into strategies, resilience, and human-centric approaches that lead to success amidst the stormy seas of innovation. With rich content and engaging narratives, this chapter serves as a compass, aiding readers in navigating the challenges posed by rapid technological evolution and emerging stronger on the shores of Digital Mastery.

CHAPTER 11
Digital Harmony - Mastering Technology in Everyday Life

In the grand tapestry of Digital Mastery, Chapter 11 unfolds as a guide to achieving digital harmony in everyday life. This chapter adopts a tech and friendly tone, weaving engaging narratives, valuable insights, and rich content to explore how individuals can master technology to enhance their daily experiences. Join us on a journey through stories, tips, and strategies that illuminate the path to seamlessly integrating technology into the fabric of everyday living.

INTRODUCTION: A SYMPHONY OF TECHNOLOGY AND DAILY LIVING

The introduction sets the stage for a harmonious exploration of how technology can be seamlessly integrated into everyday life. In a tech and friendly tone, we'll embark on a journey that envisions a symphony where technology enhances rather than overwhelms daily experiences. Engaging narratives will paint a picture of the possibilities that unfold when individuals achieve Digital Mastery in their day-to-day lives.

SECTION 1: TECH TOOLS FOR PERSONAL PRODUCTIVITY

This section explores the realm of personal productivity enhanced by tech tools. In a friendly exploration, we'll unravel narratives that showcase how individuals leverage digital tools to manage time, tasks, and goals effectively. Engaging stories will highlight instances where technology becomes a personal assistant, aiding in organization, planning, and achieving greater productivity in various aspects of life.

SECTION 2: DIGITAL WELLNESS AND MENTAL HEALTH

The narrative extends to the crucial domain of digital wellness and mental health. In a tech and friendly tone, we'll explore stories that illuminate how technology can be harnessed to promote well-being, mindfulness, and mental health. Engaging narratives will showcase instances where individuals use digital platforms, apps, and resources to foster a healthy balance between their digital and offline lives, nurturing their mental and emotional well-being.

SECTION 3: THE CONNECTED HOME AND SMART LIVING

This section delves into the concept of the connected home and smart living. In a friendly exploration, we'll unravel narratives that showcase how technology transforms living spaces into smart, connected environments. Engaging stories will highlight instances where individuals leverage smart home devices, IoT technologies, and automation to enhance convenience, energy efficiency, and overall quality of life within their homes.

SECTION 4: DIGITAL LEARNING AND CONTINUOUS GROWTH

The exploration continues into the realm of digital learning and continuous growth. In a tech and friendly tone, we'll explore stories that illustrate how individuals embrace online learning platforms, educational apps, and digital resources to expand their knowledge and skills. Engaging narratives will showcase instances where technology becomes a gateway to lifelong learning, personal development, and the pursuit of new passions.

SECTION 5: TECHNOLOGY IN RELATIONSHIPS AND SOCIAL CONNECTIONS

This section explores the role of technology in relationships and social connections. In a friendly exploration, we'll unravel narratives that showcase how individuals use digital communication tools, social media, and online platforms to nurture connections with friends, family, and communities. Engaging stories will highlight instances where technology fosters meaningful relationships, transcending physical distances and enhancing social bonds.

SECTION 6: DIGITAL CREATIVITY AND EXPRESSION

The narrative extends to the realm of digital creativity and expression. In a tech and friendly tone, we'll explore stories that illustrate how individuals leverage digital tools, platforms, and social media for creative endeavors. Engaging narratives will showcase instances where technology becomes a canvas for self-expression, artistic pursuits, and sharing creative works with a global audience.

CONCLUSION: ORCHESTRATING A DIGITAL SYMPHONY IN EVERYDAY LIFE

As we conclude this chapter, envision orchestrating a digital symphony in everyday life—a harmonious blend where technology enriches, empowers, and seamlessly integrates into the daily experiences of individuals. In a tech and friendly tone, the exploration serves as a guide, offering insights and practical tips for achieving Digital Mastery in various aspects of life. With rich content and engaging narratives, this chapter invites readers to embrace the positive potentials of technology, fostering a balanced and empowered approach to incorporating Digital Mastery into the fabric of their everyday existence.

CHAPTER 12
The Digital Tapestry - Concluding the Journey

In the final chapter of our exploration, Chapter 12 serves as the conclusion—a reflection on the intricate threads woven throughout the Digital Mastery journey. This chapter adopts a tech and friendly tone, weaving together the key insights, lessons, and visions that have emerged in the pursuit of mastering technology. Join us in this culmination as we step back to admire the digital tapestry created, celebrating the accomplishments and envisioning the possibilities that lie ahead.

INTRODUCTION: A TAPESTRY OF DIGITAL MASTERY

The introduction sets the stage for a contemplative journey, inviting readers to reflect on the intricate tapestry of Digital Mastery woven throughout the preceding chapters. In a tech and friendly tone, we'll embark on a brief exploration that encapsulates the essence of the digital journey, preparing readers for a thoughtful conclusion.

SECTION 1: KEY TAKEAWAYS AND INSIGHTS

This section delves into the key takeaways and insights garnered from the diverse chapters of the Digital Mastery exploration. In a friendly exploration, we'll unravel narratives that revisit the pivotal moments, lessons, and revelations that have shaped the understanding of technology and its role in our lives. Engaging stories will highlight the transformative power of embracing Digital Mastery as a guiding principle in navigating the digital landscape.

SECTION 2: EVOLVING PERSPECTIVES ON TECHNOLOGY

The narrative extends to evolving perspectives on technology, reflecting on how attitudes and approaches have shifted throughout the exploration. In a tech and friendly tone, we'll explore stories that showcase the dynamic nature of technology's role in shaping personal, professional, and societal landscapes. Engaging narratives will highlight instances where individuals and organizations adapt and evolve in response to technological advancements.

SECTION 3: ENVISIONING THE FUTURE OF DIGITAL MASTERY

This section invites readers to envision the future of Digital Mastery—a forward-looking exploration that sparks imagination and anticipation. In a friendly exploration, we'll unravel narratives that paint visions of a future where technology is harnessed for positive impact, innovation, and the betterment of humanity. Engaging stories will offer glimpses into potential advancements, challenges, and opportunities on the horizon.

SECTION 4: THE CALL TO ACTION

The exploration concludes with a call to action—a rallying cry for readers to take the lessons learned and insights gained from the Digital Mastery journey and apply them in their own lives. In a tech and friendly tone, we'll explore stories that showcase instances where individuals and organizations have embraced the call to action, effecting positive change, and contributing to the collective journey of mastering technology.

CONCLUSION: A GRATITUDE-FILLED FAREWELL

As we conclude this chapter and bid farewell to the Digital Mastery journey, the tone becomes one of gratitude. In a tech and friendly tone, the conclusion expresses appreciation for the readers' engagement, curiosity, and openness throughout the exploration. Engaging narratives will convey a sense of gratitude for the opportunity to embark on this digital odyssey together, weaving a tapestry of shared insights, stories, and visions.

ACKNOWLEDGMENTS: A TAPESTRY WOVEN TOGETHER

The final section extends acknowledgments—a recognition of the collaborative effort in weaving the digital tapestry of Digital Mastery. In a friendly exploration, we'll unravel narratives that express gratitude to the diverse voices, perspectives, and inspirations that have contributed to the richness of the exploration. Engaging stories will celebrate the collective endeavor that has shaped the narrative of mastering technology in the digital age.

As the digital curtain descends on this exploration, it leaves behind a tapestry—a vibrant mosaic of insights, stories, and visions that collectively embody the essence of Digital Mastery. With a tech and friendly tone, this conclusion invites readers to carry the tapestry forward, to continue the journey of mastering technology, and to embrace the boundless possibilities that await in the evolving digital landscape.